To:
With m.....
-Russ

~ Gems of Wisdom ~

Wisdom Teachings, Motivation, and Inspiration.

By Russell Kyle

Awake Publishing

Russell Kyle

To: Polly
With much love
Russ

Published by Awake Publishing
2016 USA

*W*hen the student is ready the lessons will appear. When finding yourself in a lesson, it's ok, you're ready.
If you weren't you wouldn't be in it.

~

*W*rongly judged?
We redefine the judgements made by others not through argument but through action.

~

*F*orcing life is like forcing open a flower, it only breaks. What you seek must unfold at its proper pace. It will be when it can and as it should.

~

*E*very ending is a new beginning.
Celebrate renewal by thankfully welcoming each new start.

*E*very encounter you have today has a useful purpose, take notice. When we choose to be a student of life, all things and people carry meaning-full lessons.

~

*C*areful not to mix up cause & effect. It's not what happens to us that causes our state of mind, it's our state of mind that determines the experiences we have.

~

*I*f we are not getting what we want, chances are we are getting what we need.
Trust the processes of growth & renewal.

~

*W*ant to see?
Take time daily to close your eyes
and open your Heart.

2

*T*o the degree that we let go of doubt, do we allow the miraculous to come about.

~

*H*umility is fertile ground for spiritual growth. To be humble is to be teachable. It is to be open-minded. It is to know that there is much to learn, and that everyone is our teacher.

~

*A*s you move about each day be present and take it slow, so as not to miss the countless subtle gifts popping up along the way.

~

*T*he quality of one's life is simply a matter of perspective... choose a Good one.

*C*onsider this:
If we thank God for the green lights, maybe we
should thank Him for the red ones too. For
whichever it is, good or bad, simply depends on
which side of the intersection we sit.
And so it may be with life as well. To know this
and to accept this, is 'Understanding.'

~

*Y*our thoughts are your preview of the days
coming events. Take care and choose them well

~

*T*he average person's lifespan consists of about
10 years of Mondays. Don't wish yours away.
Cherish every day.

~

*T*hrough many forms and in many ways, the
solution is always Love.

*O*pen-mindedness is humility in action. When considering another's point of view, don't be so quick to categorize it by placing it into either your 'Agree/Right' or 'Disagree/Wrong' column. Keep a 'Possibly/Not yet understood/For later review' column too.

~

*A*ction & Surrender, when used together, establish a delicate yet powerful balance. Cultivate this relationship between your taking action & your letting go.

~

*F*ollow your Heart, not your feelings, your Heart.
And If you don't know the difference, seek to know.

*T*ake care not to worry about what you may lose or may never get, or anguish over what you have lost or never had. For by this we miss the crown jewel; the awareness of the gifts we already have right now.

~

*T*rade your limitations for inspirations. When having to look forward, rather than looking forward to what may go wrong, look forward to what may go right.

~

*S*peak from your head, people will hear you with their heads. Speak from your heart, people will hear you with their hearts.

~

*C*elebrate each time you find you are wrong about something, for you've just learned something new!

*F*orgiveness is far more than just letting go of the wrong doing of another. It's about letting go of all old ideas, labels, judgements, and experiences. It's about allowing something or someone to be new and fresh, thus allowing yourself to see and experience them with new eyes. Through forgiveness a new and wonderful world comes into view.

~

*T*hat purpose one seeks comes naturally the moment that one begins shifting that occasional quiet questioning of one's own self from "What can I get?" to "How may I serve?"

~

*I*f you're waiting to for the perfect moment to make that change and it's not coming, change your idea of the perfect moment.

*W*atch what you tell yourself, you're likely to believe it.

~

*T*ruth continually moves to reveal itself. Many of our struggles are our unknowing resistance to it. We have two choices on how to go about experiencing the effects of truths revelations. We either fight, strangled by our egos fight for survival.
Or we continually let go. Ready and willing to be made anew with a quick readiness to change our minds.
The latter is the way of the student and of the wise. It is the way of understanding, the way of growth, and the way of peace.

~

What would you tell someone to encourage them, to lift them up? Now, tell these things to yourself.

*C*onsider this: Give the first 5 people who allegedly do you wrong today permission to be wrong, giving yourself a 5 person buffer between being upset and being at peace.
Take notice to how well this works today, then consider tomorrow making it 10.

~

*B*e free of the opinions of others. You need no one's approval. Your approval was validated by your very birth.

~

*T*oday has much to offer, just as is.
Consider this: Suspend your wants & desires for just one day, giving yourself permission to enjoy this day just as it is and just as it continues to unfold.

*P*erpetual Gratitude: A state of heart & mind, growing through the practice of appreciation. Cultivate gratitude. Develop a habit of periodically pausing to appreciate.

~

*G*od's uses people, whether they've chosen to participate or not.

~

*F*eeling down?
Lift someone up.

~

*L*ooking forward to something? Take care while 'looking forward' not to miss the many potentially Good moments between now & then.

*U*nlike those who divide, those who strive to unify find the Universe mimicking their actions in return. They find people and circumstance in their lives coming together in a perfect balance of purpose, companionship, and prosperity. Ask yourself often, 'Are my actions and words dividing or are they unifying?'

~

*T*ake moments to just sit and be. Leaving all distractions aside, sit and give yourself permission to do nothing for a moment or two. While there, just look around, appreciate what you see, relax, and enjoy. Do this adds space to your life. Practice often.

~

*D*o you live in a state of impending doom, or impending grace? Consider this, live with an excited and curious anticipation of what the Universe has in store for you next.

11

*A*round some next corner is a miracle with your name on it... believe it and you'll see it

~

*T*hree breaths of renewal for a new day:
1. Take a deep breath, then exhale out all the frustrations and limitations of yesterday…
2. Take a deep breath, then exhale out any fears or doubts about tomorrow...
3. Now, take a deep breath, breathing in the newness and freshness of a new day....
You are now renewed.
Have a great day!

~

*S*elf-worth isn't something one finds. Self-worth is a God given wholeness one realizes.

A Morning Prayer and Mantra:
"Thank You, thank You, thank You.
How may I serve, how may I serve, how may I
serve?"

~

*I*t is possible to be confident and still practice
humility. Be confident in the success of the
teachable, sure in the power & grace of That
which supports you.

*B*e sure to always keep 'Pray about it' and 'Just
let it go' on your list of options.

~

*T*hose who have not been there find it hard to
believe others are there, so people will talk... let
them, and just smile.

A problem's solution begins the moment we begin seeking to see its positive possibilities.

~

*T*wo steps forward and one back is still progress.

~

*W*hat matters more than where you are on your journey is the direction you are headed.

~

*G*oals are good to have, but you won't find your happiness there... only here.

~

*O*pen your eyes, for the miraculous unfolds before you.

*T*he more we can learn to appreciate the small
things, the bigger our contentment and gratitude
will grow. Develop this habit; pause often,
acknowledge the small things, and appreciate.

~

*P*ause and Appreciate.

~

*R*id yourself of preoccupation with valueless
things, ideas, fears and desires.
Focus on your blessings instead.

~

*F*orget what's wrong, pay attention to what's
right!

*I*t won't be you who will be dealing with that future event you may be fearing. It will be your future you. By the time you get there your future you likely will be ready.
So in the meantime, just relax and be present.

~

*C*riticizing and labeling others defines us, not them. We can learn much about ourselves by observing our thoughts and judgements of others.

~

*B*y our strong ideas on how others 'ought to be' we rob ourselves of the chance to know them for who they already are.
See beyond the limits of your judgements and expectations.

*O*ver concentration on trying to rearrange, fix, or think your way out of a problem, only keeps you stuck in the problem. For where your attention is so your experience is as well.

Consider this instead: Turn your attention away from the problem, focusing on anything else. If you slip, and look back, simply redirect your attention away again. This frees up the mind to find the solution. The solution won't be found in the same place, or at the same level, as the problem. Turn from the problem first. Let it go.

~

*N*one of us are perfect upon our daily challenges. When finding you've made a mistake, don't make it into a big deal. Simply acknowledge it, make amends if needed, let it go, and then begin again.

A true teacher doesn't tell you what to see, an authentic teacher simply suggests ways in which to look.
They don't insist on a destination; they simply encourage the journey.

~

*O*nly once we've learned the lesson of appreciation, only once we're thankful for all we have, only then will the Universe say, "OK, now you're ready for more."

~

*E*very experience is but a necessary step on your path. Wherever you are in your growth, on your spiritual journey, you are right where you're supposed to be... and so are they.

The mantra of the ego: 'More, more, more.'
The mantra of the spirit: 'How may I serve, how may I serve, how may I serve?'
The greatest gift one can give oneself is to give of oneself. Servant, the most revered of all positions in any spiritual community. Its benefits are most rewarding.
Serve well.

~

Some of the worst things that could have happened never happened... and you never even knew.
Be thankful for these as well.

~

We are quick to say a prayer of 'Help' when things are going bad, but let us also not forget to say a prayer of 'Thanks' when things are going well.

*H*ere's something to think about, or not.

1. Feelings are not facts.
2. You're not required to check your emotional barometer all the time... It's ok to not be ok, so you're ok.
3. You aren't your feelings, you HAVE your feelings. They aren't you. Good or bad, they're simply passing through.
4. We are usually better off than we think we are.
5. You can't believe everything you think.

~

*E*ven those alleged 'bad' days can have value and do have purpose.

~

*W*hen peace is a priority all that follows is done well, smooth, and efficient.
Be sure to add 'Time to just relax a little' to your list of things to do today.

*W*e all will one day have our last moment, our last breath. Most will have no idea while in that last moment that it is their last. Any moment could be that moment.

Would you want to live your last moments in regret of yesterday, or in fear of tomorrow, worrying of things that you feel still need done, or with people who otherwise you'd not want to be there as your last?

Live each day, each moment, each breath, as if it were your last. Continue to make good decisions for tomorrow. Yet under this awareness of the preciousness of life make your decisions on how you feel, what you cherish, what you think about, or who you choose to be around.

Whether you're taking or giving, cherishing or not, wasting moments on stress and drama or expressing gratitude and love, make these decisions based on today, this moment, as if it were your last... for it very well may be.

(Continued on next page)

(Continued)

What we leave behind that will mean most is what we contribute to this world, to our families and friends in memories of our example of how to live and be happy, how to serve others, and our personal contributions to the welfare of others. These are 'treasures stored in heaven.'
Be present. Live right. Serve others.
Enjoy and savor each moment.

*F*eeling down? There are several ways in which to lift oneself up. Two of which I discuss in my book Awakened Living.

Below is a brief description:

1. The first is helping others, "When feeling down, lift someone up." Simple, yet powerfully effective.

2. The other is the use of positive affirmations. One method I've developed and use from time to time is an 'Alphabet' version. It refocuses one's attention from self-defeating thinking to empowering and healthy thinking, just long enough until it naturally switches gears. Here is how it works:

Begin by saying to yourself (Best said aloud), "I am ____," and then fill in the blank, first with a positive word starting with the letter A, then B, and so on to Z. For example, "I am Accepting, I am Beautiful, I am Courageous, I am Delightful....." all the way to Z. (Hint for Z, 'Zealous')

Guaranteed to change your thinking, use as needed.

23

*I*t's ok to change your mind.
In fact, I highly recommend it.

~

*T*he mind should be but a stepping-stone to the
Heart, don't get stuck there.

~

*H*oarding leaves one empty. Giving fulfills.
Be a giver.
Compassion, kindness, and Love; in giving these
one lives in harmonious delight.

~

*N*ew beginnings are often disguised as painful
endings. Most all good change begins with a bit
of discomfort, so let it be instead a sign of good
things to come.

*R*ather than avoiding those who challenge you, who make you upset or uncomfortable, accept the opportunity for growth. If you really want to be free of these discomforts, if you really want these discomforts gone for good, accept the lesson. Until a lesson is learned it will not end. You may run to other people but in time whatever it is in yourself that was brought up by these people will be brought up again unless changed. These people are your opportunity to make that change. Spend time with them, learn to be around them, accept them as they are and be ok. Rather than attempting to change them or run from them, allow them to change you. Allow them to be your opportunity to cultivate understanding, acceptance and unconditional love. Don't go. Stay and accept the lesson. Once you've learned the lesson and grown as needed, and you're ok to stay, then it's ok to go.

*L*ife will never be perfect, don't waste your life
trying to make it that way.
Learn to accept life as it is, enjoying each
moment as it unfolds.

~

*B*e present. The less present we are the more we
desensitize ourselves to the goodness of life. As
we move into present moment living life comes
alive. As we are attentive to the present,
mindfully aware of our surroundings, our senses
and emotions wake up. Present moment
awareness reveals a dimension of life where we
feel more, notice more, and appreciate more,
great and small.

~

*C*ontinually let go, allowing yourself to be
moved forward.

*T*he Universe responds to your state of mind and
being. As you are, so shall you receive.

~

*D*iscard the idea of a pre-packaged spiritual
path. Consider instead a moment to moment
unfolding spiritual path.
The first is a good start, but will only allow you
to go so far. The second is boundless, a daily
invitation from you to an unlimited Source of
wisdom and goodness.
Try it all, keep what works, leaving the rest, and
following your Heart. Rely on your inspirations,
intuition, and moment to moment revelations.
Trust in the love and the guidance of that One
that created you.

~

*P*eace with others does not come by attempting
to change them, but by simply accepting them as
they are.

*R*ejoice when finding that you've been wrong, for you have just learned something new. Every correction makes us a bit wiser than we were yesterday.

~

*D*on't count your problems, count your blessings instead, no matter how small they at first may seem. For what we look for, the more of that we shall see.

~

*T*he distance between reality and your dreams is called action and faith.

~

*H*appiness is not something we get, it's something we tune into; present moment awareness and appreciation are the keys. Tune in.

*L*augh at yourself for your mistakes, apologize
when you should, let go of what you can't change
and always be kinder than you feel.

~

*M*any automatically focus first on the negative
out of habit. This only magnifies the negative
experience and often times keeps us stuck there.
But this can be changed with practice. Here is an
example of how: Let's say you're complaining
that you back is hurting. Instead of over focusing
on your back, begin to acknowledge instead that
your arms, legs and feet don't hurt; that your
lungs are clear, heart is pumping and eyes can
see, even give a prayer of thanks for these things.
Not only will this lessen the back pain, it allows
us to use the experience for good, rewiring
habitual thinking patterns. Positive thinking is a
habit developed through practice.

*T*rust fear? How many times have our fears actually come true, especially to the extent we've imagined? Rarely. So why do we continue to trust fear? Don't! Fear tells us that if we put our guard down we'll get hurt, when really it's the fear itself that hurts. The truth is that when we put our guard down, and let go of fear, we have peace. Don't trust fear, it lies, Choose peace instead.

~

*W*e get annoyed not because we are being annoyed, but because we are annoy-able. Blame only ties us to the alleged problem, acknowledge your part and be free.

~

*C*areful not to defeat yourself by being an all-or-nothing person. It's not about how far you're getting that matters, it's that you're moving and that in the right direction.

*P*ractice developing healthy habits of thought like compassion & appreciation. Any unhealthy habit of thinking can be changed with practice.

~

*T*hank-full-ness and appreciation; the two paths to satisfaction. If you're looking for it in any other way, you're only chasing shadows.

~

*J*oy and sadness come from the same seed. Each is sown with great expectations, but watered with either hope and faith or fear and doubt.
Choose well.

~

*M*anners: To encounter good manners is to feel respected and to know that some deeper part of us is being honored. Truly, none of us deserves anything less.

31

Consider allowing rather than resisting.
Choose Peace over conflict.

~

Seeking to see good in all eventually awakens
your awareness that good is all around you, all
encompassing, all the time.
Practice acknowledging good... and see.

~

People often make two mistakes in their search
of inner peace, focusing too much on the things
they cannot change and ignoring the things they
can.

~

Though you wake up each day with a purpose to
fulfill, your knowing what that purpose is isn't
always part of the plan.

*B*laming others for our being upset is a waste of time and energy. The truth is that we get upset for one underlying reason only, because we are upset-able.

~

*W*e can always point out the negative, but why enforce negative in your life or in the lives of others? Amplify the Good instead.
Perpetuate the Positive.

~

*I*f a problem can be solved, then no need to worry about it. If a problem cannot be solved, then what is the use in worrying about it?
Problem Solved!

*A*ll is possible by faith, for those things that were once thought to be beyond one's personal capabilities can now rest upon something Higher & wiser.

~

*T*ry an experiment today; Be extraordinarily kind to everyone you come in contact with and take notice at what happens... to them and to you.

~

*W*e are all well equipped to handle the matters of any one day, it's only when we try to handle more than one day at a time that we get ourselves into trouble.

~

*E*nvy is ugly. The cure: Learn to be happy for those who seem to have more, and stop counting their blessings, count yours instead.

*T*here is a greater plan, knowledge of this plan was planted in your soul at birth, so when in question, simply ask that part of you that knows.

~

*T*he moment we put as much energy into our hopes as we once did our fears, miracles happen. Use your energy wisely.

~

*T*here is purpose in everything. If you're struggling to understand what it is, then maybe that in itself is your lesson; when letting go, include your questioning 'why' as well.

~

I was recently asked, "Are your decisions based upon what you can get or what you can give? Do you feel you're a taker or a giver?" They are two good questions.

*L*ife unfolds on purpose. Some people come into our lives as blessings and others come into our lives as lessons. Each one has value.

~

*B*efore speaking one should ask oneself, will this promote fear or hope, discord or harmony, will it separate or unify, hurt or heal?

~

*T*he happy and content are not those ignoring the seeming negative parts of life, but instead those who have learned to find the lessons and value in them.

~

*S*eeing is useless when the mind is full. Stay open minded, ready to learn from moment to moment, and you'll see so much more.

When we're not 100% sure, anything is possible. The growth of open-minded and teachable; supported by their trust is something Higher, awakened by their belief in more.

~

Relax and get nothing done or obsessively get it all done so to relax? The first step in finding balance between these two is letting these ideas go, completely.

~

Discontentment is meant to be a motivator, it's a sign that great things await you, just beyond your fears. Trust this, set aside the fear, and take action.

Acceptance is the secret of contentment.
Appreciation is the secret of happiness.

~

Stay connected to your Source of Good and all
else will fall into place.

~

Humility frees the mind and opens the heart.
Learn to look with an equal eye upon all beings,
seeing the one Divine in all.

~

Despite what we tell ourselves, getting our way
won't bring comfort. It's only once we relinquish
the need to control that we obtain peace.

Worry is the result of having faith in fear, hope is the result of having faith in Good. Put your faith into something that works for you, not against you.

~

There is always a better perspective. Changing yours is but a matter of being willing to find it and take it.

~

Pain doesn't derive from the opposed, it derives from the conflict itself. Conflict cannot survive without your participation. Whatever it is, just let it go.

Recognize your ego and your fears by getting to know them. Get to know your ego's behaviors. Take notice at how the ego gets threatened and defends. Get to know your fears. Recognize your angers and moments of uneasiness as essentially deriving from fear. In seeing your ego and fears for what they are, you lessen their grip, diminish their power, and come to know at what point to simply turn away.

~

Maintain a humble heart and an open mind and you'll soon be given, every so often, glimpses beyond the veil of your concepts and understandings; you'll begin seeing a little more, growing a little wiser, understanding a little better, and believing a little deeper.

In just the right light and at just the right angle, you can see God's fingerprints on everything.

*T*he following are a few ways to develop a positive perspective: Seek to see the good in others, count your blessings often, and find the lesson in each situation.

~

*R*emember, what annoys us most in others is usually but a reflection of something we don't like in ourselves.

~

*B*e willing to honestly consider another's point of view, even if at first you don't agree. Don't be crippled by subscribing solely to your way of seeing things.

~

*E*very person you meet today has a useful purpose, take notice. When we choose to be a student of life all things and people carry meaningful lessons.

41

*K*eep your attitude clean and bright, it is the window through which you see the world.

~

*O*ften times what seems to be a discomfort is really just the Universe urging us in a better direction. Consider a new course.

~

*L*ife isn't happening to you. Life is happening for you. The Universe has a plan for you and it's good.

~

*T*hat breath you just took, that's a gift.

~

*I*f you're waiting for the perfect time and it's not coming, change your idea of the perfect time.

*O*nly by first appreciating what we have can we show the Universe we are ready for our next step up in abundance.

~

*S*elf-worth isn't a goal one achieves, it's a God-given wholeness one realizes. Your worth was validated by your very birth, with love and great purpose.

~

When tempted to argue, be silent instead. When tempted to criticize, compliment instead. When tempted to gossip, walk away instead.

~

*T*he most influence we can have on others is by being a good example.

Continually Surrender.

In freeing our minds and emotions we become more productive in our spiritual growth, and from that stem harmonious relationships, a productive life, and satisfaction with all circumstance.

~

Once a good habit of thinking is in place it naturally begins to flow. Remember that it is not by changing our outside world that we experience our inner desires, instead as we begin to change the way we see our world, the world we see changes. So choose well on your thoughts.

~

Continually re-prioritize. Set them and continually readjust as you go along. Don't beat yourself up for falling short. Just simply step back on track and proceed.

*T*oday's assignment:

Go stand in front of a mirror. Look yourself in
the eyes. Don't look away. Tell yourself the
following:

"I love you."

"I forgive you for what you've done wrong to me
and others."

"Today your limitations are behind you."

"Today you are reborn."

"Today we begin again."

Smile.

~

*J*oys are simply one side of a two-sided coin,
and so is pain.

Without both, there would be no coin. When one
comes, the other is close behind. See them both
as good; part of God's system of laws keeping a
balance to the universe. Accept them as part of
the greater Good. The more we can see this the
more "bad" and "good" will no longer be a
matter of circumstance, but instead a choice.

*L*ife. It's not a challenge to be met; it's a reality
to be experienced. Don't take things so seriously.
Laugh at yourself often. Help others to lighten up
as well.

~

*T*ake care not to waste your present moments
thinking, discussing, or trying to rewrite
yesterday or over planning, rushing or
impatiently waiting for tomorrow.
Value and live your moments, one by one.

~

*C*ontinually be aware of your motives, your
actions, and where you may owe an apology.
Watch for envy, jealousy, anger, or greed. These
are problems that begin and end only within us.
They are poisons that destroy one from the inside
out. Stay right with yourself and others.
Keep yourself right with the world and the world
will be right with you.

*H*onesty, with self, is the safety net keeping one from a fall into ignorance, ill-perception, and self-deceit.
Practice honesty.

~

*T*ake notice and give thanks.
Practice seeing and taking notice of the small blessings: a small flower in a patch of weeds, a ray of sunlight, a bird song, the sound of the wind in the trees, a friendly smile, a loving touch, a child's giggle, a bird on the windowsill, your heartbeat. Take notice and say a silent thank you for these gifts, and a silent thank you to these gifts, for their presence in your life.

~

*H*appiness doesn't come by getting what we want; it awakens while appreciating what we have.

*W*e could stand in a dark room with all the riches of the world around us and never even know. Don't. Keep the light on.
The light is appreciation.
Appreciation results from casting the light of our attention on the blessings in our lives.
Pay attention to what counts and count your blessings. Make appreciation a habit through daily practice. As we cultivate gratitude our world comes alive and is full of riches.

~

*T*o the degree that one we let go of doubt do we allow the miraculous to come about.

~

*L*ooking forward to something? Take care while 'looking forward' not to miss the many potential good moments between now and then.

Take care not to spend too much time focusing on what you don't have. Over-focusing on "not having" only attracts more "not having" into your life. Focus on having, and more and more will begin to appear.

~

Your life is your lesson. Teach well.

~

From the right perspective, it all makes sense. Faith, humility, love, and selflessness reveal this perspective.

~

Empty Yourself. We have no more room for more when full. For continued spiritual growth, every so often, lay aside all your understandings and beliefs and begin again.

*A*s you move about today, be present and take it slow, so as not to miss the countless subtle gifts popping up along the way.

~

*T*he wise often say, "I don't know."
There is wisdom in not knowing all the answers and freedom in knowing you don't have to.

~

*O*ne's next obstacle is one's next reward, simply in disguise.

~

*D*on't label your life situations.
"This is bad," or "this is good." Avoid this.
Avoid judging your life situations, it limits the possibilities. Instead, relax your resistance, knowing that the Divine is continually working for your highest Good.

50

*W*hen tempted to focus on what is wrong, pay
attention to what is right.
It has much more to offer.

~

*T*he Universe has big plans for you.
Your part? Make yourself ready; be teachable,
flexible, open-minded, and forgiving.
Freeing yourself up for positive change.

~

*B*umps in the road often occur to knock us back
on track. By these unexpected, and seemingly
unwanted, changes, we are guided and redirected
toward our highest good.

~

*I*n the practice of unconditional love and
tolerance, one's alleged enemy is really their best
teacher.

"Should haves" and "shouldn't haves" are a waste of time, they serve no good purpose and keep you stuck in the past. Make your amends, make your apologies, forgive, learn from it, and move on.

~

A good question to ask oneself often: "What could be the purpose of this person in my life, what am I to teach them, or they to teach me?"

~

*D*oes everything happen for a reason? Maybe those who can't say everything happens for a good reason will one day see that everything that does happen can be made to have a good purpose.

*H*ave an open mind.
If you want to continue to grow, always question your perceptions, and always be willing to change your mind.

~

*T*he solution can't be found at the same level as the problem. When a problem comes, first step back, let it go for a while, putting your thoughts on something positive for a bit. By this you'll be more clear-minded, emotionally centered, and better equipped to see the solution. In fact, by this, many times we find that this was itself the solution: simply letting go.

~

*T*he depth of one's anxiety measures the quality of one's spiritual condition.
Don't struggle with your problems, connect with the Solution instead.

*A*nger is a cage, the bars of its cage are blame, self-centeredness, and self-pity. Remember, justifying anger is only protecting your prison. Be free.

~

*I*t's been told by the great masters in many ways, it's one of the great inescapable governing spiritual laws: "What we serve to others, the Universe will serve to us in return." Take care and choose well

~

*T*he Spiritual journey isn't as much one of discovering the new as it is one of discarding the old. Finding your misperceptions and misunderstandings is a great victory; it is the first step to fresh and new understandings and awakenings. Always welcome new points of view, with a willingness to discard yours along the way.

Change is possible when you find you're dissatisfied with an unchangeable situation by changing your mental and emotional relation to the situation. This can be done simply by either changing your expectations on how you think things should be, or accepting things just as they already are. Simple, but not easy. Yet always possible.
Change is always an option.

~

Half of most problems are our struggling with the problem. The first step in problem solving is letting it go.

~

It's when the rough edges of others rubs up against ours that we must remember, it's a good thing, for it's a natural part of the "smoothing out of our rough edges" process.

When feeling upset that something isn't going the way you want simply shift your focus from "What's in it for me?" to "How may I serve?"

~

There is strength in softness, power in flexibility, perfection in mistakes, success in failure, clarity in confusion, and love in letting go.

~

Worry doesn't change the outcome; it only ruins the journey.
To better effect an outcome, give your all to the present moment, mentally and spiritually. Then when you do get to where you're headed, you'll be in a much better state of mind and spirit to accept the outcome, however things turn out.

*P*atience isn't having the ability to wait, it's an attitude one takes while waiting. One that says, "I'm ok with just being present and fully taking in what this moment has to offer," not rushing life, but instead trusting its natural flow.
Practice Patience.

~

*P*ay attention to the chance encounters, the synchronicities, the people you meet, the things you hear and see. They all have a message for you. When the student is ready the teachers and the lessons will appear. Be ready, alert, and pay attention.

~

*T*rue Happiness is unconditional.
Let go of the "if onlys."
The conditions we place on our happiness are the only real things between us and it.

*H*ave an idea of how your day is going to go?
Let that go, enabling you to better see what really happens.

~

*F*inding the solution.
Owning our feelings rather than blaming them on somebody else is the best position we can take in resolving our upset. For then our solution rests now within our reach, within us, not out there with them, completely out of our control.
The solution always rests with the real problem, not the alleged one.

~

*A*s we continually let go of our preconceived ideas and expectations, from moment to moment, our attention awakens, our vision clears, and a new and wonderful world begins coming into view.

*F*iguring it out? Thinking our way out of fear or anxiety doesn't work, it only adds fuel to the fire. Take care not to get caught up in this snowballing trap. Stop over thinking it and focus on the present moment instead. Settle in and rest in this state for a while, staying present, acknowledging that all is well right now. Stay disconnected from the fearful thoughts long enough until the negative emotions subside. They will. Trust the process.

~

*S*eek to see the miracles and the lessons in every encounter and every situation.
By this simple consistent practice, we tune into an awareness of God-in-action.

~

*J*ustified anger is insane. Why defend your right to be angry? Anger hurts. Your real justice is in your freedom from your anger. Let it go.

*B*e careful what you tell yourself, you're likely to believe it.
What would you tell someone to encourage them, to lift them? Now, tell these things to yourself.

~

*I*t's not what we don't have that brings feelings of lack; it's what we don't see.
Close your eyes, open your heart, and see. Count your blessings. Give thanks.

~

*H*ow is success measured? Success isn't a measurement; it's a movement and a direction. It's not about where you're at; it's about your moving in the right direction.

~

*H*umility, with an open willingness to learn and be corrected, privately or publicly, is a recipe for fulfillment and wisdom.

Parents: I think all parents want to do their best to give their children all the good experiences that life has to offer. But more importantly, I believe, to best ensure that our children have a satisfying and happy life, is to teach them to appreciate and value every person, thing and experience, great and small. From the moment life lays it at their feet to the moment life takes it away. Even at loss, once grief turns, cultivate gratitude, thankful that they experienced whatever it was, thankful that they had it, and appreciating the joy it may have brought them in that moment. Not seeing loss in despair but instead in gratitude, grateful for having had the gift, even if just for a short time.
Teach them that all of life is precious. Showing that even the tough times can become valuable lessons, and everything else, each as a gift to value and appreciate.

(Continued on next page)

(Continued)

So this is the great lesson, and we, their greatest teachers, and the greatest way to teach this most valuable way of living life? Not just by word, but more importantly by our own personal demonstrations. What they see us value, they come to value. How we express our gratitude, they too learn what and how to express. As our thankful hearts grow, theirs grow as well. As we learn, live, and demonstrate a lifestyle that places no conditions on our happiness, a life of appreciation, they too will learn what a genuinely happy life is really all about.

Take care and teach well. They are watching.

*W*hatever it is, "This too shall pass." And it will once it has taught you what you need to know.

~

*W*e worry about tomorrow, yet only with the knowledge and understanding of today.
No worries. You'll likely have what you need once you're there.

~

*B*e sure that letting go and changing direction is always on your list of options.

~

*E*xercise your gratitude.
Today, each time you find yourself looking at the clock, use it as a reminder to pause and acknowledge a blessing in that moment.
Exercise your gratitude and it'll grow.

Just as the spirit is the life of the body, giving and compassion are the life of the spirit. Giving and compassion, the outward acts of humility, keep clear the life line to the heart of your being. Study them, meditate upon them, and practice them.

~

All of creation extends teachings of understanding, all we must learn to do is pay attention and listen.

~

Confidence doesn't come from always being right, but from being OK with being wrong. There is freedom in open-mindedness. Welcome new points of view and be open to being wrong sometimes. It's OK.

Don't concern yourself with others understanding or accepting who you are or what you have to say. Be good, express good, and then watch the ripple of goodness in action.

~

Rest in a state of inner non-resistance to the flow of life, a willingness to take the necessary outward actions, and an inner detachment from the outcome.

~

Carry a curious anticipation of what God has in store for you next. Just around some next corner is a miracle with your name in it.
Believe it and you'll see it.

~

Take care on your judgments, for with them, you make your world.

*E*nough resistance and anything will break. Learn to bend so not to break. Accepting change and allowing change, by these together does one live at peace.

~

*I*t's easy to love those we like, but what about those we don't, and why would we anyways? There may be someone who doesn't like us, yet they're accepting of us, unconditionally loving us.

Love means I accept you as someone as imperfect as I am, someone who wants security and acceptance, someone who may be scared and shows it in the wrong ways, someone who is as worthy of my understanding, love, and acceptance as may feel I am of theirs. Someone who needs someone to love them first.

Morning Gratitude Shortlist
1. Woke up ✓
2. Air to breathe ✓
3. Roof over head ✓
4. Food to eat ✓
Yep, it's a Good day

~

The only difference between the value of a weed and the value of a flower, is a judgment.

~

It's not the world you're given, it's the world you see.

~

Seen in the right light, our problems are simply gifts in disguise.

67

*I*f you believe in things working out, you'll see opportunities. If you believe in things not working out, you'll see obstacles.
There is power through belief, use it wisely

~

*P*racticing deep appreciation raises our sense that we are not alone, revealing our unbreakable one on one deep connection with God and all else around us.

~

*T*he instant a problem arises its solution is born. They come and exist simultaneously. And that journey between the two; it is our lesson, our path, our growth.

~

'*P*ause and Appreciate'... use as needed.

*I*n our Western society 'goal' setting has become something we are told one should do. Yet can this be applied to spiritual growth? From some points it can be a good guide. Yet in many ways having a goal eliminates the possibility of reaching that goal. For example, let's look at present moment awareness as a goal. When being present becomes a goal, you've missed it. Making a goal is to acknowledge you're not yet there, yet you can't be 'here' if you're not 'there.' Yet even our trying happens in the moment. It's truly a journey without distance. So how to get present? First, don't make it a goal. It won't happen later, only now. Then stop trying to find it, to stay in it, and just open your eyes. You are there, here, now.

And so it is with most things spiritual, to reach the goal is to acknowledge you're already there. Consider this goal when it comes to spiritual growth: In some things, be goalless.

You are not your drama or your problems. You are not your fears or your character defects. You are not what you do or who you know, what you have or that you don't. You are not your story of what has happened to you, what is happening to you or what is to come. No, these things are but before you, and you? You are the witness to these things. The witness itself. The still and the silent, the observer of your thoughts, the observer of your feelings, the spirit that gives life to your body, that quiet watcher sitting inside. Yes, this is who you are. Remember this and live from this place, from you, that ancient peace deep within.

~

Quality over quantity. It's not about how fast you're moving as it is the direction you are headed.
And if need be, it's a great day to change direction.

*R*ather than struggling to keep up with the race, slow down and rise above it. Cultivate a stillness within: Begin a practice of daily prayer & meditation. Start today.

~

A fear of the ego is the ego's slickest trick. Fighting the ego only strengthens the ego. Keep it simple, simply turn your thoughts and attention to humility instead.

~

*S*tubborn demands, self-pity, justified anger... These leave no wiggle room for Divine intervention. Consider letting go for a bit, then notice what happens.

~

*A*ppreciation is a wonderful kind of awareness. It awakens one to the truth that what they seek has been with them all along.

71

A journey of growth is a journey without distance. It's about acceptance, clear focus, awakening, uncovering, remembering and realizing, all of which only happen in the present.

~

*A*s our faith begins to outweigh our doubts and fears, the magic begins; all the forces of the Universe begin to conspire together in a powerful, delicate, and wonderful balance for the unfolding of our most satisfying and highest good.

~

Spiritual growth isn't as much about learning as it is unlearning. It's not as much about discovering as it is uncovering.

God/Life/The Universe, gives lessons, not tests,
lessons. It's not about failing or achieving, it's
about growing. You can't fail, you can only win,
for you have no choice but grow. Your only
choice in the matter is will you grow now or will
you grow later. For the lesson will return, again
and again, until learned.
Allow it, accept it, and learn it. It's a Good thing.

~

The Universe is creating a blessing right now
with your name on it. Keep watch and pay
attention.

~

A healthy relationship is one in which each
allows the other to grow at their own pace and in
their own direction.

*B*e and remain teachable, flexible and open minded. Honestly consider all points of view, openly willing to discard yours if need be. Take care not to be too attached to the things you 'know', for each thing you 'know for sure' leaves less room for what you don't.

~

*F*eeling out of sorts often times is a sign of a good change under way.

~

*T*rust the process, let go of any attachments to the outcome, and keep your focus on today.

~

*W*as it their behavior that upset me or my expectations of their behavior? We must be willing to face the consequences of our demands and expectations.

*H*aving can feel great, until you don't. But it doesn't have to be this way.

Consider this:

All things will pass away, yet we can still enjoy them. Also there is no need to fear losing them or not having either. The key is to not get attached. To not cling to it while it moves out of your life. Learn to enjoy them as you would a good song or a sunset, thankful for the joy they bring you in that moment. Thankful that you had the experience of them in this lifetime. Gratitude, in this way, keeps the excitement in 'getting', maintains the joy in 'having', and begins to replace the pains of 'losing something' with a thankful heart of 'having had.'

~

*A*cceptance isn't about giving in to an undesirable situation. It's about knowing where you really stand, for only from here can you begin to move into something new.

Carry a 'relax & go with the flow' state of mind. As we begin accepting life's natural flow we begin understanding its purpose and trusting its direction.

~

Criticizing others defines us, not them. We can learn much about ourselves by observing our thoughts and judgements of others.
Pay attention and see.

~

Every person that shows up in our lives shows up for a reason. Seek to see the purpose and value in each encounter. What are they to offer you? What are you to offer them?

*T*here are no ordinary days.

See beyond the familiar settings and the usual schedules, seeking to see the uniqueness of each moment, the many new gifts of the day.

~

*T*he Universe can't steer until our hands are off the wheel. For best results, asking for help must be partnered with letting go.

~

*D*on't miss the new while still focusing upon the old.

~

*P*erpetual Gratitude: A state of heart and mind growing through the practice of appreciation. Periodically, pause and appreciate.

*W*e often don't see things as they are, blinded by
our ideas of how they 'ought to be.'
See beyond the limitations of your demands,
desires or expectations.

~

*T*he very fact that you woke up this morning is
proof that this day has already been
predetermined in your favor.

~

*E*ach day has much to offer. Know your goals
but keep your focus on the gifts of the journey

~

*T*he person to concern ourselves with first and
foremost is that good and kind person we should
strive to become.

*I*f you let go of what you might be, you may be pleased with who you are.

~

*U*ntil we are emptied of the old there is no room for the new. For a new perspective, simply let go of the one you hold now and your new one will come into view. No need to try to figure anything else out. Simply surrender.

~

Don't be discouraged by your human limitations, for your true nature, being spiritual, always has direct access to the unlimited wisdom and power of the Divine. All things are possible when we come from our unlimited source of Good.

~

*H*ow people treat you is on them, how you react is on you. Respond with kindness, it'll serve you well.

We experience life through our habits of thinking. The good news is we have the choice to develop new habits. All undesired thinking can be changed, with practice.

~

Life doesn't put pressure on us, we put the pressure on ourselves. As we lessen the demands we put on ourselves, peace and happiness grow. Relax and lighten up.

~

Trade your limitations for inspirations. Rather than discussing what's wrong or what could go wrong, look for and discuss what's right and what could go right. We experience our day not by the circumstances of it, but through the filter of our outlook upon it. Circumstances can't always be changed, but our outlook can. Choose a good one and have a good day.

*T*he Divine does not withhold Good. It may not come at the time or in the way you're expecting, but it's already on its way, in fact it's probably already here.

~

*I*f in a stressful situation, step back and look at the big picture, while keeping in mind, this too shall pass.
If feeling overwhelmed, look at the small picture; coming back into the present moment, while keeping in mind, first things first.

~

*C*onsider this, rather than looking for differences between others and yourself, recognize the similarities. One creates loneliness, the other emotional security.

Be the one who gives everyone the benefit of the doubt, who refuses to cosign someone else's complaining, who always points out the positive point of view.

~

People are naturally drawn to those who lift others up, rather than those who only glorify themselves. Ego repels, humility attracts. Take care and choose well.

~

A continual renewing of one's spiritual practices opens new channels, awakens new understandings, and ignites new joys. Try something new and different this week.

*T*he way of the Divine isn't one of punishment or fear, but one of love and forgiveness. Come to know these, to express these, and you'll come to know the Divine.

~

*W*e are always in a lesson: A bad or good situation, interrupted plans, a stroke of good luck, a stranger's smile, a traffic jam, a flower.
Pay attention.

~

*S*truggling with a choice is really struggling with the fear of potential unwanted consequences. Once we are willing to accept the consequences of our choices, choosing will no longer be a struggle.

*T*roubled? Consider this: Let go, even if just for the rest of today. Give yourself permission to let go, then see how it looks come tomorrow.

~

*T*ake care that your 'wants' don't blind you from your 'haves.' Fully appreciate what you have first, only then will the door to more open, for by this we are showing the Universe that we can gratefully handle prosperity.

~

*I*f something isn't meant to be, it won't. If it is, it will. Maybe instead of trying to change things, we might just practice a little acceptance instead.

Let go of the need to defend yourself. Only pride
needs defense. Why defend pride?
The part of you that deserves your attention
needs no defense, focus there.

~

When you feel you've exhausted all possibilities,
remember this, you haven't.
Tune in to your source of Good, reconnect, relax,
and simply begin again.

~

Our first step in resolving anger is to not take the
actions of others personally. More than likely
their actions have more to do with them than they
do with you. The next is to find the part you
played in the anger, whether it actually be in the
situation, or whether it be within yourself; your
fears, expectations or prejudices. Admitting our
part is our first step in resolving the situation and
our first step toward peace.

*D*o you possess your things or do your things possess you? Having things is Ok, being overly attached to those things can be a problem. For all things will pass, good and bad.

~

*I*f you want to continue to grow, always question your perceptions, and always be willing to change your mind.

~

*I*t's better to make use of a chance to change rather than try to change the chance. Change is inevitable, but change is good... when we allow it. Allow it.

*I*f speech is silver, silence is gold. When you
must speak, speak just a few words, kind and
soft. Want to be heard? This is the way to reach a
listener's ear.

~

I can't say that everything happens for a good
reason, but I can say
for sure, that everything that does happen can be
made to have a good
purpose.

~

*C*onsider showing others the same respect,
kindness, forgiveness and understanding that
you'd expect others to give you.

No matter what your ego may tell you, the truth
is, when you criticize or
say something negative about someone, it makes
you look bad.

~

Low self-esteem and insecurities often arise
from ones need to be seen as, or to be, perfect.
Let this go and just be yourself. Only then will
you truly feel secure.

~

Love and tolerance tires out its opposition. Love
others until they can learn to love themselves.

Keep a spark in your spiritual life.
Keep a spark in your spiritual life by continually
renewing your ideas and beliefs on God, life and
the laws of good.
Continually explore new points of view, careful
not to get too attached to just one. Many will
grab your attention at just the moment they
should, as a stepping stone for your continued
awakening, but take it in and then let it go. Take
care to learn and experience what you can and
then move on. In my experience I return to some
of these old understandings and ideas, from time
to time, from a new point of view, and see more,
but to have this happen I had to first move on.
Read new books, go to different spiritual retreats,
conventions or rituals, talk to many people,
inquire with an open mind, try new meditations,
explore new forms of connecting with Good, new
ways to give and help others, explore religions,
spiritual beliefs, but all with an open mind.
All this while continually letting go, of even your
newest of understandings, allowing your next
step up in understanding.

For correspondence with the author you may email him at Aw8kning@aol.com

Made in the USA
Charleston, SC
14 January 2016